Hidden
surprise
CAKES

CONTENTS

INTRODUCTION

It's the latest baking trend sweeping the Internet and one that will have everyone gasping in amazement. Using a variety of clever techniques, we've created a selection of sensational cakes and cupcakes that look just like any other on the outside, but as soon as you cut a slice from a cake or bite into a cupcake, a delightful hidden surprise is revealed. From a mighty multicolored layered Rainbow Cake to a Party Piñata Cake bursting with candies, a spiced Halloween loaf with a black bat in each slice or a frosted cupcake fizzing with popping candy, there's a cake here for every occasion. Some are quick and easy to make, while others need a little more time and skill, but each recipe has clear and concise instructions with detailed step-by-step pictures to guide you. These cakes are fun to make and will certainly keep everyone guessing—it's up to you whether you give away the secret!

TECHNIQUES

HIDDEN CAKE SHAPES WITHIN CAKES

Although time-consuming to make, these cakes really do have the ultimate wow factor. The technique is simple, if a little fussy, but once you've perfected it, you can experiment with a whole variety of shapes in different themes as well as a range of colors. Cleverly created by concealing a row or circle of already-baked cake shapes within the yellow cake batter before baking, the two secrets to success are to keep the shaped cake design fairly simple and to make sure that the shapes are placed as closely together as possible when they go back in the cake pan for the final bake. The stunning Polka-Dot Cake on page 46 and the Hidden Heart Cupcakes on page 68 are the easiest cakes to make using this method, so perhaps try one of these recipes first.

LAYERED OR PATTERNED YELLOW CAKES

Coloring yellow cake batter is an effective way to create impact for a special celebration cake. From layered rainbow colors to subtle shaded ombre cakes they are really easy to make. You will find that the batter is able to take plenty of food coloring—after baking, the surface of the cakes may be a little moister than usual but this won't affect the taste of the finished cake. To create a patterned cake, such as the Chocolate Surprise Cake on page 16, different colors or flavors of batter are piped into the cake pan before baking. The pattern will be different every time, but that makes them even more fun to bake.

CHECKERBOARD DESIGN

Accurate cutting and careful reassembly is needed to give this style of cake a professional finish. Once you've perfected the basic technique, try experimenting with different color or flavor combinations.

CAKES WITH GOODIES INSIDE

Children will be delighted to find candies, chocolates, or popping candy inside cakes and cupcakes, and this simple technique can be used to make more sophisticated cakes, too, such as the Tumbling Berries Cake on page 58. These filled cakes are best baked a day or two in advance, then filled and decorated on the day of serving.

BASIC CAKE BATTERS

Most of the cakes in this book are based on a classic yellow, or sponge, cake batter made with all-purpose flour, baking powder, butter, sugar, and eggs. Some are made using the all-in-one method, where all the ingredients are beaten together until pale and creamy. To avoid the layer cakes being too domed, the baking powder has been reduced from some recipes.

Where a firmer batter is needed to hold the hidden cake shapes in place, a pound cake-style batter is used. These cakes need to be cooked at a lower temperature and for a lot longer than usual. To check if they are cooked all the way through, gently push a toothpick right down to the bottom of the cake, avoiding the area where the baked cake shapes are placed.

ESSENTIAL EQUIPMENT

As well as all the usual baking paraphernalia, such as bowls, spoons, sifters, strainers, parchment paper, paper cupcake liners, and measuring spoons and cups, here's a brief guide to some of the more vital pieces of equipment you will need to create these stunning cakes.

CAKE PANS

It's worth investing in a selection of good-quality cake pans that will last for years. Loose-bottom ones make light work of removing the baked cakes from the pans. Many of the cakes in this book are made in shallow cake pans ranging from 6 to 8 inches in diameter. You may already have a couple of each size, and they are easy to find online and in the kitchen section of large department stores. For cakes that have more than two layers, simply bake in batches, cleaning, regreasing, and relining the cake pans each time—or just borrow a couple of extra pans from a friend. To avoid wobbly cakes, do make sure the pans you use are all exactly the same size!

SILICONE MOLDS

Silicone bakeware is flexible, lightweight, and easy to store and clean, but the range of sizes is not as extensive as it is for metal bakeware. However, to make the Polka-Dot Cake on page 46, you will need a couple of deep round cake molds and a cake pop mold, and for the Birthday Surprise Giant Cupcake on page 74, you'll need a giant cupcake silicone mold. You should be able to find all the molds online or in large department stores or kitchenware retailers. Thoroughly clean the molds in warm, soapy water and make sure they are completely dry before storing.

LARGE MEASURING CUP

Many of the recipes in this book will require the batter to be divided equally to ensure perfectly proportioned layers. When measuring liquids—including the batter—make sure the cup is placed on a flat surface and that you bend down so the measuring marks on the cup are at eye level.

ELECTRIC MIXER

Although this is not completely essential, few of us will make a cake nowadays without the help of a time-saving electric mixer. A handheld one with two or three speed settings is ideal. A free-standing mixer will be more expensive, but it will give you time to get on with other preparations and is especially useful for all-in-one cake batters and making large quantities of buttercream.

SPATULAS

A selection of flexible silicone spatulas is ideal for making cakes. You can use a spatula to help when dividing quantities of batters into separate bowls without any wastage. For the perfect finish to filled and frosted cakes, a long, flexible spatula is essential for spreading both frostings and fillings. You may find a smaller straight or angled spatula will also be useful when gently smoothing cake batter around already-baked cake shapes.

PASTRY BAGS AND TIP

Large, disposable plastic pastry bags are reasonably priced and save time when piping swirls and rosettes on cakes and cupcakes. They also come in handy for some of the recipes where the cake batter is piped evenly around the already-baked cake shapes. Large or medium star-shape tips are required for the swirls and rosettes and a medium plain tip will be needed for piping cake batter. For intricate fine piping, you can make a small pastry bag from a triangular sheet of parchment paper.

CUTTERS

A selection of round metal cutters in various sizes will be useful for cutting and decorating cakes. For cakes that have an already-baked cake shape inside, you'll need to buy a specific cutter, such as a palm tree or heart shape. Cake decorating specialty suppliers usually have a good range of shapes and sizes. Make sure that the shaped cutter is not too large and will fit comfortably inside the cake pan.

WORKING WITH FOOD COLORINGS

Many of the really amazing creations in this book, such as the Rainbow Cake on page 12 and the Tropical Sunrise Cake on page 60, are made with colored cake batters. To give the batter a good strong color without affecting the consistency it's best to use edible coloring pastes or gels. These are available in a whole kaleidoscope of colors, from pale pastels to bright primaries, from cake supply retailers and online.

Add the coloring sparingly at first and mix in gently but thoroughly to avoid any streaks in the baked cake. You'll find the cakes that need a good strong color will take a lot of paste or gel, but try not to overbeat the cake batter or the baked cake will have a dense and heavy texture.

FROSTINGS

Nearly all the cakes in this book are decorated with one of these quick-and-easy frostings in varying quantities.

>> BUTTERCREAM

This classic sweet, buttery frosting is easy to work with and is perfect for sandwiching together and decorating yellow cakes. Simply made using butter and confectioners' sugar and flavored with vanilla, it will keep for up to a week in the refrigerator.
This recipe makes 1 quantity (2 cups).

Ingredients

1½ sticks unsalted butter, softened

2¾ cups confectioners' sugar

1 teaspoon vanilla extract

1 tablespoon hot water

1. Place the butter in a large bowl and beat with a handheld electric mixer for 2–3 minutes, until soft and pale.

2. Sift in half the confectioners' sugar and mix with a wooden spoon until blended with the butter. Sift in the remaining confectioners' sugar and mix again.

3. Add the vanilla extract and beat for 2–3 minutes, or until the mixture is smooth, pale, and creamy. Add the hot water and beat for an additional 30 seconds to give the buttercream a silky smooth texture.

VARIATIONS

Chocolate: Blend 2 tablespoons of unsweetened cocoa powder with 2 tablespoons of boiling water to make a smooth paste. Let cool for a few minutes, then beat into the buttercream.

Almond: Replace the vanilla extract with almond extract.

Lemon or orange: Replace the vanilla extract with 2 tablespoons of lemon juice or orange juice. Add some finely grated lemon zest or orange zest to the buttercream, if desired.

TIP

To color buttercream, add a little food coloring paste or gel with the tip of a toothpick and beat in thoroughly to create an even color.

>> GLOSSY CHOCOLATE FROSTING

Rich, smooth, and intensely chocolaty, this frosting has a wonderful glossy finish and spreads well. Use a good-quality baking chocolate, preferably with 50–70 percent cocoa solids. This recipe makes 1 quantity (1⅓ cups).

Ingredients

6 ounces semisweet chocolate, broken into pieces

1 stick butter, diced

½ cup heavy cream

1. Put the chocolate and butter in a large heatproof bowl. Set the bowl over a saucepan of simmering water, making sure the bottom of the bowl doesn't touch the water, and heat until the chocolate and butter have melted.

2. Remove the bowl from the heat and stir the mixture until smooth. Let cool for 2–3 minutes, then stir in the cream. Let stand at room temperature for 20–30 minutes, then chill in the refrigerator for 40–50 minutes, stirring occasionally, until thick enough to spread.

VARIATIONS

Mocha: Dissolve 1 teaspoon of coffee granules in 1 tablespoon of boiling water. Let cool, then add to the heatproof bowl with the chocolate and diced butter.

Mint: Stir a few drops of peppermint extract into the melted mixture with the cream.

Orange: Add ½–1 teaspoon of pure orange extract to the melted mixture with the cream.

>> CREAM CHEESE FROSTING

This tangy frosting has a wonderful smooth, light consistency and is perfect for spreading over rich chocolate cakes or piping in generous swirls on top of cupcakes. It will keep in the refrigerator for a couple of days. This recipe makes 1 quantity (1½ cups).

Ingredients

½ cup cream cheese

4 tablespoons unsalted butter, softened

½ teaspoon vanilla extract

1 cup confectioners' sugar, sifted

1. Beat the cream cheese and butter together in a mixing bowl with a wooden spoon until smooth and thoroughly blended.

2. Beat in the vanilla extract, then sift in the confectioners' sugar and beat again until the frosting is smooth and creamy. Chill in the refrigerator until required.

VARIATIONS

Orange or lemon: Replace the vanilla extract with 1 teaspoon of orange juice or lemon juice and add 2 teaspoons of finely grated orange zest or lemon zest, if desired.

>> MASCARPONE CREAM FROSTING

This delicious frosting has a wonderful texture and goes perfectly with fresh fruit. This recipe makes 1 quantity (2 cups).

Ingredients

1 cup mascarpone cheese

3 tablespoons confectioners' sugar, sifted

1 cup heavy cream

1. Place the mascarpone cheese in a large bowl and beat with a wooden spoon until very smooth.

2. Beat in the confectioners' sugar, then gradually beat in the cream.

VARIATIONS

Lemon: Add 2 teaspoons of finely grated lemon zest and a few drops of lemon extract.

Coffee: Beat in 2 teaspoons of coffee extract with the cream.

DECORATING TIPS AND TECHNIQUES

Once you've created your special surprise-inside cake, it's definitely worth taking a little time to apply the frosting and decorations. Follow these hints and tips to get the perfect finish every time.

Chilling cakes in the refrigerator or the freezer for a short while will help to create a firm cake to work on. It won't affect the flavor or texture of the cake as long as you bring the cake back to room temperature before serving.

Before you start, make sure that the frosting is the correct consistency. If it's too soft to hold its shape, chill it in the refrigerator for a little while. If it's too firm, it will be difficult to spread smoothly, so you'll need to let it stand at room temperature to soften slightly.

Spreading an initial, thin layer of buttercream or cream cheese frosting onto the cake, sometimes called a "crumb coat," will help to seal in any loose crumbs. Use a spatula and don't worry if the cake looks messy—after chilling the coated cake, you'll apply a thicker layer of frosting, which will cover any crumbs and imperfections. Wipe the spatula clean frequently to avoid getting crumbs in the bowl of frosting.

Be generous when applying the thicker layer of frosting and work quickly. For a smooth finish, hold the spatula almost flat to the side of the cake and use a sweeping motion all around it (using a cake turntable will help you to get a really smooth finish). To add texture, use the tip of the spatula to create swirls or ridges around the side and top of the cake.

Piping swirls of frosting on cakes and cupcakes is a quick-and-easy way to decorate cakes and looks really impressive. If you haven't piped before, make extra frosting and do a practice run before you start on the cake. To pipe large swirls, pipe two or three decreasing circles of frosting, gently lifting the pastry bag as you work. For rosettes or rose swirls, start piping from the center and pipe two or three circles in a tight spiral pattern close to the surface of the cake or cupcake.

STORAGE

Cakes that are filled and frosted with buttercream or glossy chocolate frosting will keep well in an airtight container in a cool place (not the refrigerator) for three or four days.

Cakes with a cream cheese frosting or fresh cream coating will need to be kept in the refrigerator and are best eaten within two days. Remove from the refrigerator 20–30 minutes before serving.

Cakes that have candies or fruits hidden inside them are best eaten on the day of filling, although the cakes can be made two or three days in advance.

All the plain cakes will freeze well for up to one month. Make sure they are completely cold before wrapping in aluminum foil. Thaw at room temperature before filling and frosting.

RAINBOW CAKE

This cake has the ultimate "wow" factor, with a kaleidoscope of rainbow colored layers all smothered in sweet vanilla buttercream. It's the perfect party cake.

Serves 12-14 >> **Prep time:** 50 mins, plus time to cool & chill >> **Cooking time:** 40–44 mins

Red, orange & yellow cakes

2 cups all-purpose flour

2¼ teaspoons baking powder

2 sticks butter, softened, plus extra for greasing

1¼ cups granulated sugar

5 extra-large eggs

red, orange, and yellow food coloring pastes or gels

Green, blue & violet cakes

2 cups all-purpose flour

2¼ teaspoons baking powder

2 sticks butter, softened, plus extra for greasing

1¼ cups granulated sugar

5 extra-large eggs

green, blue, and violet food coloring pastes or gels

To decorate

2 quantities of buttercream (see page 8)

2 teaspoons rainbow-colored sugar sprinkles

You will also need

three 8-inch round cake pans

1. Preheat the oven to 350°F. Grease three 8-inch round cake pans and line the bottoms with parchment paper.

2. To make the red, orange, and yellow cake layers, sift together the flour and baking powder into a large bowl and add the butter, sugar, and eggs. Beat with a handheld electric mixer for 1–2 minutes, until smooth and creamy. Using a large measuring cup, divide the batter equally among three separate bowls.

3. Beat enough red, orange, and yellow food coloring paste into each bowl of batter to produce a good strong color (see step 3 photograph).

4. Spoon the batters into the prepared pans and gently level the surfaces. Bake in the preheated oven for 20–22 minutes, or until risen and just firm to the touch. Let cool in the pans for 10 minutes, then turn out onto a wire rack and let cool completely. Do not turn off the oven.

5. Clean the pans, then grease them again and line the bottoms with parchment paper. Make and bake the green, blue, and violet cake layers in the same way as you did the red, yellow, and orange layers.

6. To decorate, spread ⅓ cup of the buttercream on each of the cake layers except the red one. Place the violet layer on a board and then carefully stack the remaining layers on top, finishing with the red layer (see step 6 photograph).

CONTINUED

3

6

7

8

RAINBOW
CAKE CONTINUED...

7. Spread some of the buttercream in a thin layer around the sides and over the top of the cake. Chill the cake in the refrigerator for 30 minutes (see step 7 photograph).

8. Spread the remaining buttercream around the sides and top of the cake, smoothing the sides with a spatula (see step 8 photograph). Make slight ridges in the buttercream on the top of the cake with the tip of the spatula, then sprinkle with the sugar sprinkles.

Tip
Be bold when adding the food coloring to the separate cake batters to achieve a really vibrant, colorful cake.

CHOCOLATE SURPRISE CAKE

Take a slice from this demure looking cake to reveal a surprise all chocoholics will love—a chocolate flavored pattern running through it!

Serves 8 >> **Prep time:** 1 hour, plus time to cool >> **Cooking time:** 30–35 mins

2 tablespoons unsweetened cocoa powder

2 tablespoons hot water

2 cups all-purpose flour

2 teaspoons baking powder

2 sticks butter, softened, plus extra for greasing

1¼ cups granulated sugar

5 extra-large eggs

1 teaspoon vanilla extract

2 tablespoons milk

To decorate
1 quantity pink buttercream (see page 8)

2 teaspoons grated semisweet chocolate

You will also need
two 7-inch round cake pans

large disposable pastry bag fitted with a large plain tip

2 small disposable pastry bags

1. Preheat the oven to 350°F. Grease two 7-inch round cake pans and line the bottoms with parchment paper.

2. Mix the cocoa powder with the water in a small bowl to make a smooth paste and set aside. Sift the flour and baking powder into a large bowl and add the butter, sugar, eggs, and vanilla extract. Beat with a handheld electric mixer for 1–2 minutes, until smooth and creamy.

3. Put about 1 cup of the vanilla batter into a separate bowl and beat in 1 teaspoon of the chocolate paste to produce a pale brown color. Put another 2 cups of the vanilla batter into a second bowl and beat in the remaining cocoa paste to produce a dark brown color. Beat the milk into the remaining vanilla batter (see step 3 photograph).

4. Spread a thin layer of the milk vanilla batter in the bottom of each prepared pan and gently level the surface with a spatula (see step 4 photograph). Spoon the remaining milk vanilla batter into a large disposable pastry bag fitted with a large plain tip. Spoon the two colored batters into smaller disposable pastry bags and snip off the ends.

5. Pipe some of the dark brown batter into each prepared pan in two concentric rings, each about 1 inch wide. Pipe a thinner line of light brown batter along the center of each dark brown ring (see step 5 photograph).

CONTINUED

3

4

5

6

7

9

CHOCOLATE SURPRISE CAKE CONTINUED...

6. Pipe the remaining dark brown batter over the light brown batter to cover it as much as possible (see step 6 photograph).

7. Pipe the remaining vanilla batter in between the chocolate rings and evenly over the top, then gently level the surfaces with a spatula (see step 7 photograph).

8. Bake in the preheated oven for 30–35 minutes, or until risen, golden, and just firm to the touch. Let cool in the pans for 10 minutes, then turn out onto a wire rack and let cool completely.

9. To decorate, sandwich the two layers together with some of the buttercream and spread the remainder around the sides and over the top of the cake, smoothing and swirling it with a spatula (see step 9 photograph). Sprinkle with the grated chocolate to decorate.

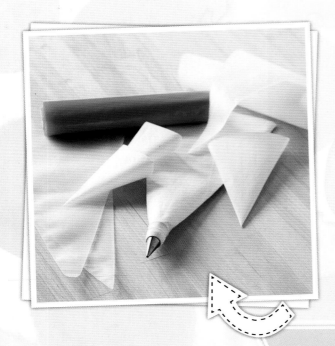

Tip

Don't worry if your piping of the two chocolate batters is a little erratic—the pattern does not need to be too uniform and will probably be different each time you make it.

LADYBUG CUPCAKES

Bite inside these cute ladybug cupcakes and you'll find a brightly colored red cake dotted with delicious chocolate polka dots!

Makes 12 >> **Prep time:** 40 mins, plus time to cool >> **Cooking time:** 20–25 mins

1 stick butter, softened

²/₃ cup granulated sugar

2 eggs, beaten

1 cup all-purpose flour

1¼ teaspoons baking powder

red food coloring paste or gel

¹/₃ cup semisweet chocolate chips

To decorate

1 quantity green buttercream
(see page 8)

4 ounces red ready-to-roll fondant

2 ounces black ready-to-use fondant

boiled water, cooled

tubes of black and white
writing icing

You will also need

12-section muffin pan

large pastry bag fitted with
a medium star tip

1. Preheat the oven to 350°F. Line a 12-section muffin pan with paper liners.

2. To make the cupcakes, put all the ingredients (except for the food coloring and chocolate chips) into a large bowl and beat with a handheld electric mixer for 1–2 minutes, until smooth and creamy. Beat in enough red food coloring paste to give the batter a bright red color.

3. Place a spoonful of the cake batter in the bottom of each paper liner, then sprinkle with half the chocolate chips. Spoon the remaining cake batter over the top and then sprinkle with the remaining chocolate chips (see step 3 photograph).

4. Bake in the preheated oven for 20–25 minutes, or until risen and just firm to the touch. Transfer to a wire rack and let cool completely.

5. To decorate, spoon the buttercream into a large pastry bag fitted with a medium star tip. Pipe stars all over the top of each cupcake to cover completely (see step 5 photograph).

6. To make the ladybugs, evenly divide the red fondant into 12 pieces. Shape each piece into an oval to form the bodies. Shape 12 small pieces of black fondant into flat ovals for the faces and attach to the bodies with a dab of the water (see step 6 photograph). Roll tiny pieces of black fondant into dots and attach to the bodies to resemble the ladybugs' spots. Score down the back of each body with a knife to mark the wings. Use the black and white writing fondant to make eyes on the faces.

3

5

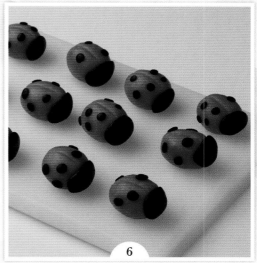

6

Tip

You can make the ladybugs a few days in advance. Let stand on a board, uncovered, for 3–4 hours, until they are dry, then store in an airtight container for up to one week.

CHECKERBOARD CAKE

Moist mocha- and orange-flavored cakes are simply cut into rings and reassembled to create this stunning checkerboard effect.

Serves 12 >> **Prep time:** 1 hr 15 mins, plus time to cool & chill >> **Cooking time:** 1 hr

Chocolate cake

2 tablespoons unsweetened cocoa powder

1 teaspoon instant coffee granules

2 tablespoons hot water

1¾ cups all-purpose flour

1¾ teaspoons baking powder

2 sticks butter, softened, plus extra for greasing

1 cup granulated sugar

4 eggs

¼ cup ground almonds

2 tablespoons milk

Orange cake

1¾ cups all-purpose flour

1¾ teaspoons baking powder

2 sticks butter, softened

1 cup granulated sugar

4 eggs

⅓ cup ground almonds

2 tablespoons orange juice

To decorate

1 quantity glossy chocolate frosting (see page 9)

2–3 tablespoons white chocolate and semisweet chocolate chips

You will also need

two 7-inch round cake pans

2½-inch round metal cutter

4½-inch saucer

1. Preheat the oven to 350°F. Grease two 7-inch round cake pans and line the bottoms with parchment paper.

2. To make the chocolate cake, mix together the cocoa powder, coffee granules, and hot water in a small bowl to make a smooth paste. Set aside. Sift the flour and baking powder into a large bowl and add the butter, sugar, eggs, ground almonds, and milk. Beat with a handheld electric mixer for 1–2 minutes, until smooth and creamy, then beat in the cocoa paste.

3. Divide the batter evenly between the prepared pans (see step 3 photograph) and bake in the preheated oven for 30 minutes, or until risen and just firm to the touch. Let cool in the pans for 10 minutes, then turn out onto a wire rack and let cool completely. Do not turn off the oven. Clean the pans, then grease and line the bottoms with parchment paper.

4. To make the orange cake, sift the flour and baking powder into a large bowl and add the butter, sugar, eggs, and ground almonds. Beat with a handheld electric mixer for 1–2 minutes, until smooth and creamy, then beat in the orange juice.

5. Divide the batter evenly between the prepared pans and bake in the preheated oven for 25–30 minutes, or until risen and just firm to the touch. Let cool in the pans for 10 minutes, then turn out onto a wire rack and let cool completely.

CONTINUED

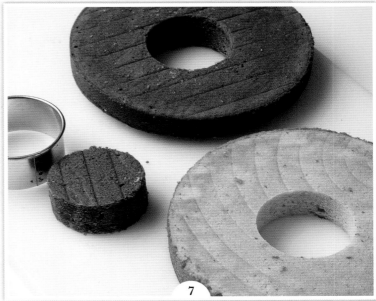

6. Place the cold cakes in the freezer and let chill for about 30 minutes, until firm. Place the chilled cakes on two large boards. If the tops of the cakes are slightly uneven, use a serrated knife to level them.

7. Using a 2½-inch round metal cutter, stamp out a circle from the center of each cake and carefully remove (see step 7 photograph).

8. Then, using a 4½-inch saucer as a guide, cut a ring of cake from each layer. Very carefully separate and remove the rings, leaving four outer rings of cake (see step 8 photograph).

9. Reassemble the cakes, swapping the chocolate and orange cake circles and rings so you end up with four layer cakes that look like targets (see step 9 photograph). Handle the rings carefully to prevent them from cracking.

10. To decorate, spread a thin layer of frosting over one of the cake layers and top with a second alternate cake layer (see step 10 photograph). Repeat to stack up all the layers neatly, making sure you alternate the layers as you work to produce a checkerboard appearance when you cut into the cake.

11. Spread the remaining frosting in an even layer around the sides and over the top of the cake, smoothing it with a spatula (see step 11 photograph). Decorate the top and around the bottom edges of the cake with chocolate chips.

Tip

Don't chill the cakes in the freezer for too long or they may crack when you cut them into rings. If they have become too firm, let stand at room temperature for 5–10 minutes.

RED VELVET CHEESECAKE CAKE

This indulgent cake makes an ideal party dessert, with a rich and creamy layer of baked vanilla cheesecake sandwiched between two classic red velvet sponge cakes.

 Serves 12 >> **Prep time:** 1 hr, plus time to cool & chill>> **Cooking time:** 1 hr 5 mins

Cheesecake

1³⁄₄ cups cream cheese

¹⁄₃ cup granulated sugar

1 teaspoon vanilla extract

2 eggs, beaten

¹⁄₂ cup sour cream

1 tablespoon cornstarch

Red velvet cakes

1²⁄₃ cups all-purpose flour

1¹⁄₂ teaspoons baking soda

3 tablespoons unsweetened cocoa powder

1¹⁄₂ sticks butter, softened, plus extra for greasing

1 cup granulated sugar

2 eggs, beaten

²⁄₃ cup buttermilk

1 teaspoon vanilla extract

2 tablespoons red liquid food coloring

To decorate

1 quantity cream cheese frosting (see page 10)

2 ounces semisweet chocolate, melted

You will also need

7-inch round springform pan

two 7-inch round cake pans

small paper pastry bag

1. Preheat the oven to 325°F. Grease a 7-inch round springform pan and line the bottom with parchment paper. Wrap a layer of aluminum foil around the bottom and up the sides of the pan and place it on a baking sheet.

2. To make the cheesecake, place the cream cheese, sugar, and vanilla extract in a large bowl and beat together until smooth. Gradually beat in the eggs, then add the sour cream and cornstarch, stirring until smooth.

3. Spoon the batter into the prepared pan and gently level the surface. Bake in the preheated oven for 35 minutes, or until just set but still slightly wobbly in the center. Turn off the oven and let the cheesecake cool in the oven with the door ajar. When it has cooled completely, cover the top of the pan with a sheet of parchment paper and place it in the refrigerator for at least 4 hours or overnight.

4. To make the red velvet cake layers, preheat the oven to 350°F. Grease two 7-inch round cake pans and line the bottoms with parchment paper. Sift together the flour, baking soda, and cocoa powder into a bowl and set aside.

5. Place the butter and sugar in a large bowl and beat together with a handheld electric mixer until pale and fluffy. Gradually beat in the eggs, then beat in the buttermilk, vanilla extract, and food coloring. Fold in the sifted flour mixture (see step 5 photograph).

CONTINUED

6. Divide the batter evenly between the prepared pans and level the surfaces. Bake in the preheated oven for 30 minutes, or until risen and just firm to the touch. Let cool in the pans for 10 minutes, then turn out onto a wire rack and let cool completely.

7. Unclip and remove the springform sides from the cheesecake. Place one red velvet cake on top of the cheesecake (see step 7 photograph).

8. Invert the cake with the cheesecake onto a board or serving plate and carefully remove the bottom of the pan and the lining paper. Gently place the second cake on top (see step 8 photograph).

9. Spread a thin layer of the frosting around the sides and over the top of the layered cake. Place in the refrigerator for 30 minutes.

10. Spread the remaining frosting all over the cake, smoothing it lightly with a spatula (see step 10 photograph). Spoon the melted chocolate into a small paper pastry bag. Snip off the end and pipe swirls on top of the cake. Chill in the refrigerator until ready to serve.

Tip

To melt chocolate, break the chocolate into pieces and place in a large heatproof bowl. Set the bowl over a saucepan of simmering water, making sure the bowl does not touch the water, and heat until the chocolate has melted. Remove the bowl from the pan and stir the chocolate until smooth.

POPPING CANDY CUPCAKES

These cupcakes will certainly set the taste buds tingling with a secret surprise of cracking popping candy tucked away inside.

Makes 12 >> **Prep time:** 20 mins, plus time to cool >> **Cooking time:** 15–20 mins

1 cup all-purpose flour

1¼ teaspoons baking powder

1 stick butter, softened

⅔ cup granulated sugar

2 extra-large eggs, beaten

½ teaspoon vanilla extract

1 tablespoon milk

pink food coloring paste or gel

1½ oz popping candy

To decorate
1 quantity pink buttercream
(see page 8)

pink edible cake decorating glitter

You will also need
12-section muffin pan

large pastry bag fitted with a large star tip

1. Preheat the oven to 350°F. Line a 12-section muffin pan with paper liners.

2. Sift together the flour and baking powder into a large bowl. Add the butter, sugar, eggs, vanilla extract, and milk. Beat with a handheld electric mixer for 1–2 minutes, until smooth and creamy. Beat in enough food coloring to give the batter a mid-pink color (see step 2 photograph).

3. Divide the batter evenly among the paper liners (see step 3 photograph). Bake in the preheated oven for 15–20 minutes, or until risen, golden, and firm to the touch. Transfer to a wire rack and let cool.

4. Use a small serrated knife to cut a cone shape out of the center of each cupcake. Place about 1 teaspoon of popping candy into each hollow. Slice off the tip of each cone shape, then replace the cones on top of the popping candy to cover completely (see step 4 photograph).

5. To decorate, spoon the buttercream into a large pastry bag fitted with a large star tip. Pipe swirls of frosting on top of each cupcake and sprinkle with pink cake decorating glitter.

Tip
You can make the cupcakes a day in advance or freeze them for up to two months, but only fill and frost just before serving or the candy will lose its "pop."

PINK OMBRE CAKE

With both sponge and frosting delicately shaded from dark to light pink, this cake has a sophisticated look. You can vary the color choices as you please—shades of purple, blue, orange, or yellow all work well.

Serves **10** >> **Prep time:** 1 hr, plus time to cool & chill >> **Cooking time:** 15–18 mins

1¾ cups all-purpose flour

2¼ teaspoons baking powder

2 sticks butter, softened, plus extra for greasing

1¼ cups granulated sugar

4 extra-large eggs

2 tablespoons milk

2 teaspoons rose water

pink food coloring paste or gel

To decorate

1½ quantity buttercream (see page 8)

pink food coloring paste or gel

1 tablespoon edible sugar pearls

You will also need

four 7-inch round cake pans

1. Preheat the oven to 350°F. Grease four 7-inch round cake pans and line the bottoms with parchment paper.

2. Sift together the flour and baking powder into a large mixing bowl and add the butter, sugar, eggs, milk, and rose water. Beat with a handheld electric mixer for 1–2 minutes, until pale and creamy (see step 2 photograph). Divide the batter equally among four bowls.

3. Beat increasing amounts of pink food coloring paste into each of the bowls of batter to produce four distinctly different shades of pink from pale to bright (see step 3 photograph). Spoon each bowl of batter into a prepared pan and gently level the surface.

4. Bake in the preheated oven for 15–18 minutes, or until risen and just firm to the touch. Let cool in the pans for 5 minutes, then turn out onto two wire racks and let cool completely.

5. To decorate, use one-quarter of the buttercream to sandwich the four cake layers together. Start with the darkest pink layer at the bottom and finish with the lightest pink layer on top (see step 5 photograph). Spread a thin layer of the buttercream around the sides and over the top of the cake and chill in the refrigerator for 30 minutes.

6. Place half of the remaining buttercream in a smaller bowl and add enough pink coloring paste to produce a pale pink color. Divide the remaining buttercream between two small bowls and color one half mid-pink and the other half bright pink (see step 6 photograph).

CONTINUED

7. Using a spatula, spread the bright pink buttercream around the sides of the bottom third of the assembled cake. Spread the mid-pink buttercream around the middle of the cake, merging it a little with the bright pink buttercream (see step 7 photograph).

8. Spread the pale pink buttercream around the sides of the top of the cake, merging it a little with the mid-pink buttercream. Spread the remaining pale pink buttercream over the top of the cake, swirling it with the spatula (see step 8 photograph). Sprinkle the sugar pearls over the top just before serving.

Tip

If you only have two pans, make the cakes in two batches, but reserve a little of the colored batters from the first batch so you can match the shading.

HIDDEN HEARTS CAKE

Slice into this wonderful almond-flavored layer cake to discover tiny marzipan hearts. It's the perfect way to say "I love you" to someone special.

Serves 8 >> **Prep time:** 45 mins, plus time to cool >> **Cooking time:** 25–30 mins

2 sticks butter, softened,
plus extra for greasing

1¼ cups granulated sugar

4 extra-large eggs, beaten

1¾ cups all-purpose flour

1¾ teaspoons baking powder

1 teaspoon almond extract

1 tablespoon milk

To decorate

confectioners' sugar, for dusting

8 ounces natural marzipan

red food coloring paste

1 quantity buttercream,
(see page 8)

You will also need

two 8-inch round cake pans

thin metal barbecue skewer

small heart-shaped cutter

1. Preheat the oven to 350°F. Grease two 8-inch round cake pans and line the bottoms with parchment paper.

2. Place the butter and sugar in a bowl and beat together until pale and creamy. Gradually beat in the eggs, adding a spoonful of the flour if the mixture starts to curdle. Sift in the flour and baking powder and gently fold in, using a metal spoon. Fold in the almond extract and milk.

3. Divide the batter evenly between the prepared pans and level the surfaces. Bake in the preheated oven for 25–30 minutes, or until risen, golden, and just firm to the touch. Let cool in the tins for 10 minutes, then turn out onto a wire rack and let cool completely.

4. To decorate, lightly dust a surface with confectioners' sugar, then knead the marzipan until smooth. Knead in enough food coloring paste to color the marzipan bright red.

5. Take just over one-quarter of the marzipan and thinly roll out to a 14-inch long roll. Then take just under one-quarter of the marzipan and roll to an 8-inch long roll (see step 5 photograph).

6. Form the rolls into heart shapes by first scoring along the length of each roll with a knife. Run a thin metal skewer along the scored lines to shape the top of the heart. Turn the rolls over and pinch along the length of each roll to shape the pointed bottom of the heart (see step 6 photograph).

CONTINUED

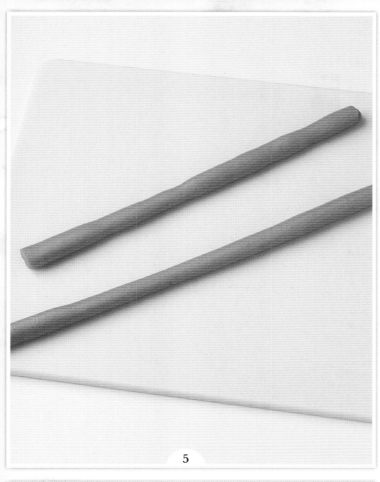

5

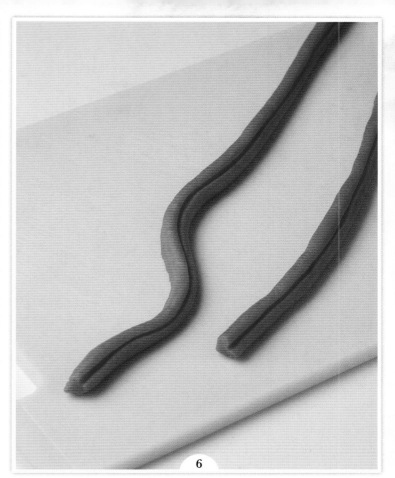

6

7

8

7. Spread one-third of the buttercream on one of the layers. Arrange the heart-shape rolls, point side down, in two concentric circles on the buttercream, pressing them down gently (see step 7 photograph). Spread another third of the buttercream over the marzipan rolls in an even layer. Place the second cake layer on top.

8. Spread the remaining buttercream over the top of the cake, swirling it into circles with the tip of a spatula. Thinly roll out the remaining marzipan on a surface lightly dusted with confectioners' sugar. Use a small heart-shape cutter to stamp out eight marzipan hearts and arrange them on the top of the cake (see step 8 photograph).

Tip
To color the marzipan, dip a toothpick into the food coloring paste and transfer it to the marzipan. Knead in and repeat until you have the depth of color you require.

COOKIES & CREAM CUPCAKES

These delicious cupcakes are packed with crushed chocolate cookies and have a great crisp cookie bottom, too. Topped with swirls of tangy cream cheese frosting, they won't be around for long.

 Makes 12 >> **Prep time:** 20 mins, plus time to cool >> **Cooking time:** 20–25 mins

20 round chocolate sandwich cookies

1 stick butter, softened

²/₃ cup granulated sugar

2 extra-large eggs, beaten

1 cup all-purpose flour

1 teaspoon baking powder

½ teaspoon vanilla extract

1 tablespoon milk

To decorate

2 quantities cream cheese frosting, chilled (see page 10)

14 round mini chocolate sandwich cookies

- -

You will also need

12-section muffin pan

large pastry bag fitted with a large star tip

1. Preheat the oven to 350°F. Line a 12-section muffin pan with paper liners and place a cookie in the bottom of each liner (see step 1 photograph). Coarsely chop the remaining cookies and set aside.

2. Place the butter and sugar in a bowl and beat until pale and creamy. Gradually beat in the eggs, adding a spoonful of the flour if the mixture starts to curdle. Sift in the flour and baking powder and fold in gently, using a metal spoon. Fold in the vanilla extract, milk, and chopped cookies.

3. Divide the batter evenly among the paper liners (see step 3 photograph). Bake in the preheated oven for 20–25 minutes, or until risen, golden, and firm to the touch. Transfer to a wire rack and let cool.

4. To decorate, spoon the frosting into a large pastry bag fitted with a large star tip. Pipe swirls of frosting on top of each cupcake and top each with a mini cookie (see step 4 photograph).

5. Halve the remaining mini cookies, discard the cream filling, then finely crush the cookies and sprinkle the crumbs over the frosting.

Tip

Don't chop the cookies too finely; you want to have nice big chunks in the batter.

BABY BOY OR GIRL CAKE

This is a fun, edible way to reveal whether you are expecting a new baby boy or girl—just fill the center of the cake with pink or blue candies.

Serves **8** >> ***Prep time:*** 1 hr, plus time to cool >> ***Cooking time:*** 25–30 mins

1¾ cups all-purpose flour

2¼ teaspoons baking powder

2 sticks butter, plus extra
for greasing

1¼ cups granulated sugar

4 eggs

1 teaspoon vanilla extract

To decorate

⅓ quantity buttercream
(see page 8)

6 ounces pink or blue candies, such
as sugar-coated chocolate drops or
sugared almonds

1 pound white ready-to-use fondant

confectioners' sugar, for dusting

baby blue and pink food coloring
paste or gel

You will also need

three 6-inch round cake pans

2¾-inch round metal cutter

small round cutter

small paintbrush

1. Preheat the oven to 350°F. Grease three 6-inch round cake pans and line the bottoms with parchment paper.

2. Sift together the flour and baking powder into a large bowl. Add the butter, sugar, eggs, and vanilla extract and beat with a handheld electric mixer for 1–2 minutes, until smooth and creamy. Divide the batter equally among the prepared pans. Gently level the surfaces.

3. Bake in the preheated oven for 25–30 minutes, or until risen and just firm to the touch. Let cool in the pans for 10 minutes, then turn out onto a wire rack and let cool completely.

4. To assemble, use a 2¾-inch round metal cutter to stamp out a circle from the center of one of the cake layers to make a ring. Press the cutter into the center of the other two cake layers to a depth of about ½ inch and scoop out some of the cake to make a dip in the center of each layer (see step 4 photograph).

5. Place one of the whole layers (dip side up) on a board and spread one-quarter of the buttercream all around the rim of the dip. Place the cake ring on top. Spread another quarter of the buttercream over this cake.

6. Fill the hollow with pink or blue candies (see step 6 photograph). Place the second whole cake layer on top (dip side down). Spread the remaining buttercream in a thin layer around the sides and over the top of the cake.

CONTINUED

4

6

7

9

7. Roll out the fondant on a surface lightly dusted with confectioners' sugar to a 14-inch circle. Gently lift the fondant onto a rolling pin and drape it over the cake, allowing it to fall down the sides (see step 7 photograph). Gently smooth out any folds and creases with your hands. Trim off the excess fondant with a small knife.

8. Reknead the fondant scraps until smooth and divide in two. Use the blue and pink coloring paste to color one half of the fondant baby blue and the other half pale pink.

9. Thinly roll out each piece of fondant on a surface lightly dusted with confectioners' sugar and use a small round cutter to stamp out small circles—about 15 of each color. Attach the circles to the cake in a random design with a dampened paintbrush (see step 9 photograph).

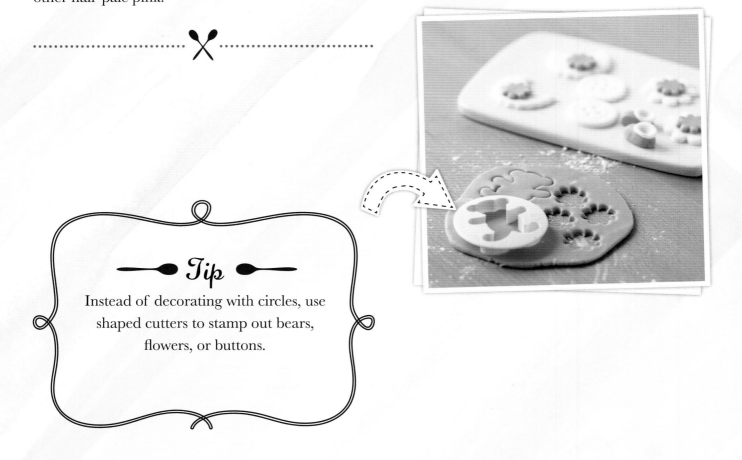

Tip

Instead of decorating with circles, use shaped cutters to stamp out bears, flowers, or buttons.

POLKA-DOT CAKE

Amaze your guests with this incredible chocolate cake studded inside with vibrant blue cake polka dots. It's much easier to make than you may think—you just need to invest in a cake pop mold.

Serves 10 >> **Prep time:** 1 hr 30 mins, plus time to cool >> **Cooking time:** 1 hr

Blue cake

¾ cup all-purpose flour, sifted

¾ teaspoon baking powder

1 stick butter, softened, plus extra for greasing

½ cup granulated sugar

2 eggs

blue food coloring paste or gel

Chocolate cake

1²⁄₃ cups all-purpose flour

1½ teaspoons baking powder

⅓ cup unsweetened cocoa powder

2 sticks butter, softened, plus extra for greasing

1 cup granulated sugar

4 extra-large eggs

¼ cup milk

To decorate

1 quantity glossy chocolate frosting (see page 9)

blue sugar-coated chocolate drops

You will also need

20-section silicone cake pop mold

two 6½-inch round silicone cake molds

1. Preheat the oven to 350°F. Lightly grease both halves of a 20-section silicone cake pop mold and place the bottom mold on a baking sheet.

2. To make the blue cake for the balls, place the flour, baking powder, butter, sugar, and eggs in a large bowl and beat with a handheld electric mixer for 1–2 minutes, until smooth and creamy. Beat in enough of the food coloring paste to give the batter a bright blue color (see step 2 photograph).

3. Use a teaspoon to distribute the batter evenly in the bottom mold, being careful to avoid overfilling each dip in the cake mold (see step 3 photograph). Now place the other mold on top. Bake in the preheated oven for 20 minutes, or until the cake balls are risen and firm to the touch. Let the cakes cool in the molds for 20 minutes, then carefully remove them, trimming off any excess cake around the balls with the tip of a small knife. Transfer to a wire rack and let cool completely. Do not turn off the oven.

4. To make the chocolate layers, sift together the flour, baking powder, and cocoa powder into a large bowl and add the butter, sugar, and eggs. Beat with a handheld electric mixer for 1–2 minutes, until smooth and creamy, then beat in the milk (see step 4 photograph).

5. Grease two 6½-inch round silicone cake molds and place on a large baking sheet. Divide the chocolate cake batter in two. Spread one-third of each quantity in the bottom of each silicone mold. Arrange ten sponge balls in each mold, placing one in the center and the remaining nine in a circle (see step 5 photograph).

CONTINUED

POLKA DOT
CAKE CONTINUED...

6. Spoon the remainder of each batter into each cake mold, making sure the batter goes down around the sides of the cake balls. Gently level the surface with a spatula (see step 6 photograph).

7. Bake in the preheated oven for 35–40 minutes, or until the cakes are risen and just firm to the touch. Let cool in the molds for 10 minutes, then carefully turn out onto a wire rack and let cool completely.

8. To decorate, sandwich the two cake layers together with one-quarter of the frosting. Spread the remaining frosting around the sides and over the top of the cake, smoothing and swirling it with a spatula (see step 8 photograph). Gently press the sugar-coated chocolate drops around the edge of the top of the cake.

Tip

Try using a different color for the cake balls inside, or divide the cake batter among bowls and use three or four different colors for a rainbow effect.

NEAPOLITAN CAKE

This colorful cake will make a stunning centerpiece for a summer afternoon treat with layers of chocolate, strawberry, and vanilla cake covered in swirls of pink and white frosting.

 Serves 10 >> **Prep time:** 1 hr, plus time to cool & chill >> **Cooking time:** 25–30 mins

1½ tablespoons cocoa powder, sifted

1½ tablespoons hot water

1¾ cups all-purpose flour

2¼ teaspoons baking powder

2 sticks butter, softened,
plus extra for greasing

1 cup granulated sugar

4 eggs

2 tablespoons milk

½ teaspoon vanilla extract

½ teaspoon strawberry extract

pink food coloring paste or gel

To decorate

1½ quantities buttercream
(see page 8)

pink food coloring paste or gel

You will also need

three 6-inch round cake pans

large pastry bag fitted with
a medium star tip

1. Preheat the oven to 350°F. Grease three 6-inch round cake pans and line the bottoms with parchment paper. Mix together the cocoa powder and hot water in a small bowl to make a smooth paste and set aside.

2. Sift together the flour and baking powder into a large bowl and add the butter, sugar, eggs, and milk. Beat with a handheld electric mixer for 1–2 minutes, until smooth and creamy (see step 2 photograph). Divide the batter equally into three separate bowls.

3. Beat the chocolate paste into one bowl of batter. Beat the vanilla extract into the second bowl of batter. Beat the strawberry extract and enough food coloring to produce a bright pink color into the third bowl of batter.

4. Spoon the batters into the prepared pans and gently level the surfaces. Bake in the preheated oven for 25 minutes, or until risen and just firm to the touch. The chocolate layer may need an extra 4–5 minutes. Let cool in the pans for 10 minutes, then turn out onto a wire rack and let cool completely (see step 4 photograph).

5. To decorate, use some of the buttercream to sandwich the three cake layers together, with the chocolate layer at the bottom and the vanilla layer at the top (see step 5 photograph). Spread a thin layer of buttercream around the sides and over the top of the stacked layers. Place in the refrigerator for 30 minutes.

6. Divide the remaining buttercream between two bowls. Use the pink food coloring to color one bowl of buttercream deep pink. Use a spatula to spoon the pink buttercream down one side of a large pastry bag fitted with a medium star tip. Spoon the white buttercream down the other side of the pastry bag.

7. Starting at the bottom, pipe three rosettes of buttercream up the side of the cake. Repeat all around the cake until the sides are completely covered (see step 7 photograph). Pipe rosettes in concentric circles over the top of the cake.

Tip

For a simpler decoration, use a half quantity of buttercream to sandwich and cover the cakes, spreading the buttercream smooth with a spatula. Press rows of pink, white, and milk chocolate disks onto the sides and top of the cake.

HALLOWEEN BAT CAKE

This is the ideal cake to make for a spooky Halloween party. The scary surprise inside this cake will keep trick-or-treaters guessing all evening.

 Serves 8 >> **Prep time:** 1 hr 10 mins, plus time to cool & chill >> **Cooking time:** 1 hr 25 mins–1 hr 45 mins

Black cake

1 cup all-purpose flour

1¼ teaspoons baking powder

1 stick butter, softened, plus extra for greasing

²⁄₃ cup granulated sugar

2 extra-large eggs

1 tablespoon black food coloring paste or gel

Spiced cake

1²⁄₃ cups all-purpose flour, sifted

1½ teaspoons baking powder

1½ sticks butter, softened, plus extra for greasing

½ cup granulated sugar

⅓ cup firmly packed light brown sugar

3 eggs

2 tablespoons maple syrup

1 teaspoon allspice

To decorate

1 quantity cream cheese frosting (see page 10)

You will also need

9 x 5 x 3-inch loaf pan

bat-shape cookie cutter

1. Preheat the oven to 350°F. Grease a 9 x 5 x 3-inch loaf pan and line the bottom and two long sides with parchment paper.

2. To make the black cake for the bats, put the flour, baking powder, butter, sugar, and eggs into a large bowl and beat with a handheld electric mixer for 1–2 minutes, until smooth and creamy. Beat in the black food coloring.

3. Spoon the batter into the prepared pan and level the surface. Bake in the preheated oven for 30–40 minutes, or until risen, firm to the touch, and a toothpick inserted into the middle of the cake comes out clean. Let cool in the pan for 10 minutes, then turn out onto a wire rack and let cool completely. Turn off the oven. Clean the pan, then grease and line the bottom and two long sides with parchment paper.

4. When the cake is completely cold, use a serrated knife to cut it into ten even slices (see step 4 photograph). Arrange cut side down on a board and place in the freezer for about 25 minutes.

5. Meanwhile, preheat the oven to 325°F.

6. To make the spiced cake, put all the ingredients into a large bowl and beat together with a handheld electric mixer for 1–2 minutes, until smooth and creamy. Spoon about half the batter into the prepared pan and use a spatula to angle the batter up one side of the pan (see step 6 photograph).

CONTINUED

7. Use a bat-shape cookie cutter to stamp out ten bat shapes from the chilled black cake slices (see step 7 photograph).

8. Arrange the bat shapes along the length of batter in the cake pan, making sure the slices line up at the same angle and are as close together as possible (see step 8 photograph).

9. Spoon the remaining spiced cake batter into the pan, spooning it around and over the bat shapes to cover them completely (see step 9 photograph). Gently level the surface.

10. Bake in the preheated oven for 55 minutes–1 hour 5 minutes, or until the cake is risen and golden and a toothpick inserted into the middle of the cake comes out clean. Let cool in the pan for 15 minutes, then transfer to a wire rack and let cool completely.

11. To decorate, use a spatula to spread the cream cheese frosting over the top of the cold cake (see step 11 photograph).

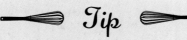
Tip

If you want to decorate your cake with a Halloween theme, make simple pumpkin decorations with orange fondant and green jelly candies.

TUMBLING BERRIES CAKE

This cake is a delicious variation on a summertime cake with sweet juicy berries hidden inside just ready to come bursting out. Serve with extra berries or a fresh fruit sauce for a special dessert.

Serves **12** >> **Prep time:** 45 mins, plus time to cool & chill >> **Cooking time:** 25–30 mins

3 sticks butter, softened,
plus extra for greasing

1¾ cups granulated sugar

6 eggs, beaten

2¾ cups all-purpose flour

2¾ teaspoons baking powder

1 teaspoon vanilla extract

2 tablespoons milk

Filling & decoration

1 quantity mascarpone cream
frosting (see page 10)

2 cups mixed summer berries, such
as raspberries, blueberries, small
hulled strawberries, and red currants

You will also need

three 8-inch round cake pans

5½-inch saucer

1. Preheat the oven to 350°F. Grease three 8-inch round cake pans and line the bottoms with parchment paper.

2. Put the butter and sugar in a bowl and beat together until pale and creamy. Gradually beat in the eggs, adding a spoonful of the flour if the mixture starts to curdle. Sift in the flour and baking powder and gently fold in, using a metal spoon. Fold in the vanilla extract and milk.

3. Divide the batter among the prepared pans and gently level the surfaces. Bake in the preheated oven for 25–30 minutes, or until risen and just firm to the touch. Let cool in the pans for 10 minutes, then turn out onto a wire rack and let cool completely.

4. To fill and decorate the cake, cut out the center of one of the cake layers, using a 5½-inch saucer as a guide, to make a ring. Place one whole cake on a board and spread some of the frosting around the cake in a 1¼-inch border. Place the cake with the center removed on top (see step 4 photograph).

5. Fill the center of the middle cake with two-thirds of the berries (see step 5 photograph). Spread some more of the frosting around the rim of the middle cake. Gently place the second whole cake on top.

6. Spread some of the remaining frosting in a thin layer around the sides of the cake. Chill the cake in the refrigerator for 15 minutes.

7. Spread two-thirds of the remaining frosting around the sides of the cake, smoothing it into vertical lines with the tip of a small spatula (see step 7 photograph). Spread the remaining frosting over the top of the cake and decorate with the remaining berries.

4

5

7

Tip

The cake layers can be made a day in advance or frozen for up to two months, but only assemble and decorate a few hours before serving.

TROPICAL SUNRISE CAKE

Be prepared for gasps of wonder when you slice into this cake. It's a real work of art, yet it is surprisingly easy to create when you know the secret technique.

Serves 10 >> **Prep time:** 1 hr 15 mins, plus time to cool & chill >> **Cooking time:** 2 hrs 5 mins–2 hrs 15 mins

Chocolate cake

1¼ cups all-purpose flour

1¾ teaspoons baking powder

¼ cup unsweetened cocoa powder

1½ sticks butter, softened, plus extra for greasing

¾ cup granulated sugar

3 extra-large eggs

Sunset cake

1⅔ cups all-purpose flour, sifted

1½ teaspoons baking powder

1½ sticks butter, softened

¾ cup granulated sugar

3 extra-large eggs

2 tablespoons milk

red, orange, and yellow food coloring pastes or gel

To decorate

½ quantity glossy chocolate frosting (see page 9)

- -

You will also need

9 x 5 x 3-inch loaf pan

palm-tree-shape cookie cutter

1. Preheat the oven to 350°F. Grease a 9 x 5 x 3-inch loaf pan and line the bottom and two long sides with parchment paper.

2. To make the chocolate cake for the palm trees, sift together the flour, baking powder, and cocoa powder into a large bowl and add the butter, sugar, and eggs. Beat with a handheld electric mixer for 1–2 minutes, until smooth and creamy.

3. Spoon the batter into the prepared pan and level the surface. Bake in the preheated oven for 45–50 minutes, or until risen, firm to the touch, and a toothpick inserted into the middle of the cake comes out clean. Let cool in the pan for 10 minutes, then turn out onto a wire rack and let cool completely. Turn off the oven.

4. When the cake has cooled completely, use a serrated knife to cut it into 8 even-size slices. Arrange cut side down on a board and place in the freezer for 30 minutes. When the slices are firm, use a palm-tree-shape cookie cutter to stamp out eight chocolate cake palm trees (see step 4 photograph). Return to the freezer for an additional 20–30 minutes, or until firm.

5. Meanwhile, preheat the oven to 325°F. Clean and grease the loaf pan and line the bottom and two long sides with parchment paper.

CONTINUED

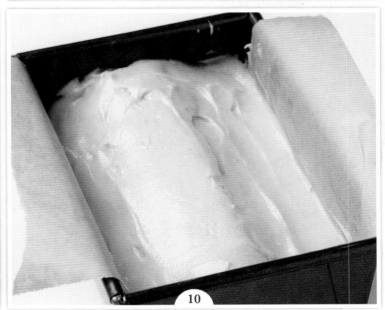

6. To make the sunset cake, put all the ingredients (except the food colorings) into a large bowl and beat with a handheld electric mixer for 1–2 minutes, until smooth and creamy. Divide the batter into three bowls of roughly equal quantities. Use the coloring pastes to color one bowl of batter pale red, one orange, and one yellow (see step 6 photograph).

7. Spoon the pale red batter into the bottom of the prepared pan in an even layer. Spoon just over half the orange batter along the length of half the pan (see step 7 photograph).

8. Arrange the chilled chocolate palm trees along the length of the batter in the pan, making sure the slices line up at the same angle and are as close together as possible (see step 8 photograph).

9. When all the palm trees are in the pan, spoon the remaining orange batter over the tree trunks (see step 9 photograph).

10. Spoon the yellow batter over the palm trees to cover them completely. Use a small angled spatula to gently spread the batter, being careful to avoid knocking the palm trees over (see step 10 photograph).

11. Bake in the preheated oven for 1 hour 20 minutes–1 hour 25 minutes, or until the cake is risen and golden and a toothpick inserted into the middle of the cake comes out clean. Loosely cover the top with aluminum foil after 1 hour 10 minutes if the top of the cake is becoming too brown. Let cool in the pan for 15 minutes, then turn out onto a wire rack and let cool completely.

12. To decorate, use a spatula to spread the glossy chocolate frosting in a thick layer over the top of the cold cake.

Tip

Try and place the palm trees as close together as possible to stop the cake batter from bubbling up through them when the cake is baked.

CHRISTMAS TREE WREATH CAKE

Celebrate the festive season with this delightful themed cake with the added surprise of Christmas tree cake running through the middle. Make sure the cookie cutter is ½ inch shorter than the depth of the pan.

Serves 16 >> **Prep time:** 1 hr, plus time to cool & chill >> **Cooking time:** 1 hr 45 mins–1 hr 55 mins

Green cake

1¾ cups all-purpose flour, plus extra for dusting

2 teaspoons baking powder

2 sticks butter, softened, plus extra for greasing

1 cup granulated sugar

4 extra-large eggs

green food coloring paste or gel

Vanilla cake

2 cups all-purpose flour, sifted

2 teaspoons baking powder

2 sticks butter, softened

1 cup granulated sugar

4 extra-large eggs

1 teaspoon vanilla extract

To decorate

1 quantity buttercream (see page 8)

2 teaspoon red, white, and green confetti sugar sprinkles

1 teaspoon edible silver balls (optional)

You will also need

3-inch deep 2-quart tube pan

2½-inch-tall Christmas-tree-shape cookie cutter

large disposable pastry bag fitted with a medium plain tip

1. Preheat the oven to 325°F. Thoroughly grease a 2-quart tube pan (at least 3 inches deep), then lightly dust with flour.

2. To make the green cake for the Christmas trees, put the flour, baking powder, butter, sugar, and eggs into a large bowl and beat with a handheld electric mixer for 1–2 minutes, until smooth and creamy. Beat in enough green food coloring paste to give the batter a Christmas tree-green color.

3. Spoon the batter into the prepared pan and level the surface. Bake in the preheated oven for 45–50 minutes, or until risen, firm to the touch, and a toothpick inserted into the middle of the cake comes out clean. Let cool in the pan for 10 minutes, then turn out carefully onto a wire rack and let cool completely. Turn off the oven.

4. When the cake is completely cold, place it on a board and use a serrated knife to cut it into 16 wedge-shape slices (see step 4 photograph). Slightly separate the slices (still maintaining the tube shape), then place in the freezer for 30 minutes.

5. Use a 2½-inch tall Christmas-tree-shape cookie cutter to stamp out 16 Christmas tree shapes from the chilled cake wedges. Re-form the trees into the tube shape again (see step 5 photograph) and return to the freezer for an additional 30–40 minutes, or until firm.

6. Meanwhile, preheat the oven to 325°F. Clean the pan, thoroughly grease, and lightly dust with flour.

CONTINUED

7. To make the vanilla cake, put all the ingredients into a large bowl and beat with a handheld electric mixer for 1–2 minutes, until smooth and creamy. Spoon the batter into a large disposable pastry bag fitted with a medium plain tip.

8. Pipe three lines of batter into the bottom of the prepared pan, then continue piping the batter up the sides of the center of pan and smooth with a spatula (see step 8 photograph).

9. Take two Christmas tree cake shapes together and gently place them in the vanilla batter, pointed side down and leaning into the center of the pan. Repeat with the remaining slices, keeping them as close together as possible to reform the tube shape (upside down) inside the pan (see step 9 photograph).

10. Pipe the remaining vanilla batter around the other sides of the trees and over the tops to cover them completely (see step 10 photograph). Gently level the surface.

11. Bake in the preheated oven for 45 minutes, then loosely cover the top of the cake with aluminum foil. Bake for an additional 15–20 minutes, or until a toothpick inserted into the cake comes out clean (make sure to place the toothpick right into the cake in an area where there is more vanilla cake). Let cool in the pan for 15 minutes. Run a small angled spatula around the sides of the cake, carefully turn out onto a wire rack, and let cool completely.

12. To decorate, spread some of the buttercream in a thin layer all over the cake. Chill the cake in the refrigerator for 30 minutes. Spread the remaining buttercream all over the cake, swirling it with a spatula (see step 12 photograph). Decorate the top of the cake with confetti sprinkles and edible silver balls, if using.

Tip

Once you have the technique perfected, why not try a different hidden shape, such as a star or gingerbread man? Just make sure the cutter is small enough to fit inside the cake pan.

HIDDEN HEARTS CUPCAKES

These beautiful chocolate cupcakes have a pink cake heart nestling inside them. Perfect to give as a Valentine's Day treat wrapped in a cupcake gift box.

 Makes 12 >> **Prep time:** 40 mins, plus time to cool & chill >> **Cooking time:** 40–45 mins

Pink cake

¾ cup all-purpose flour

1 teaspoon baking powder

1 stick butter, softened, plus extra for greasing

½ cup granulated sugar

2 eggs

pink food coloring paste or gel

Chocolate cake

1¼ cups all-purpose flour

¼ cup unsweetened cocoa powder

1½ teaspoons baking powder

1½ sticks butter, softened

¾ cup granulated sugar

3 eggs

1 tablespoon milk

To decorate

1 quantity buttercream (see page 8)

1 tablespoon heart-shape red or pink sugar sprinkles

....

You will also need

7-inch round cake pan

1½-inch wide heart-shape cutter

12-section muffin pan

large disposable pastry bag fitted with a large plain tip

1. Preheat the oven to 350°F. Grease a 7-inch round cake pan and line the bottom with parchment paper.

2. To make the pink cake for the hearts, put the flour, baking powder, butter, sugar, and eggs into a large bowl and beat with a handheld electric mixer for 1–2 minutes, until smooth and creamy. Beat in enough of the pink food coloring to color the batter deep pink (see step 2 photograph).

3. Spoon the batter into the prepared pan and level the surface. Bake in the preheated oven for 20–25 minutes, or until risen and just firm to the touch. Let cool in the pan for 10 minutes, then turn out onto a wire rack and let cool completely. Turn off the oven.

4. When the cake has cooled completely, transfer it to a board and place it in the freezer for about 30 minutes.

5. Use a 1½-inch wide heart-shape cutter to stamp out 12 heart shapes from the chilled cake (see step 5 photograph). Return the heart cakes to the freezer and freeze for an additional 30 minutes. Meanwhile, preheat the oven to 350°F. Line a 12-section muffin pan with muffin cups.

6. To make the chocolate cake, put all the ingredients into a large bowl and beat with a handheld electric mixer for 1–2 minutes, until smooth and creamy.

CONTINUED

2

5

7

8

7. Place a spoonful of chocolate cake batter in the bottom of each muffin cup, then gently place a chilled pink cake heart upright on the batter (see step 7 photograph).

8. Spoon the remaining chocolate cake batter into a large disposable pastry bag fitted with a large plain tip. Pipe the batter around the hearts and use the tip of a spatula to spread the batter to cover the top of the hearts as much as possible (see step 8 photograph).

9. Bake in the preheated oven for 20 minutes, or until risen and just firm to the touch. Transfer to a wire rack and let cool completely.

10. To decorate, use a spatula to swirl the buttercream over the tops of the cupcakes. Sprinkle with heart-shape sugar sprinkles.

Tip

To be sure that you see the heart shape when you cut into the cupcakes, mark a line on the underside of each muffin cup. Put all the hearts in the same direction of the line and check the bottoms of the baked cupcakes before cutting.

PIÑATA PARTY CAKE

Children will love the candy surprise hidden inside this stunning cake, and adults will marvel at how it was made. Make both cakes a day in advance so that they have time to become firm before you scoop.

Serves **10–12** >> *Prep time:* 1 hr 15 mins, plus cooling & chilling >> *Cooking time:* 1 hr 10 mins–1 hr 20 mins

4 sticks butter, softened,
plus extra for greasing

2¼ cups granulated sugar

8 extra-large eggs, beaten

4½ cups all-purpose flour

3½ teaspoons baking powder

¼ cup milk

10 ounces mixed candies such as jelly beans and sugar-coated chocolate drops

2 tablespoons pastel-colored confetti sugar sprinkles

To decorate
1 quantity buttercream (see page 8)

You will also need
two 2-quart round ovenproof bowls

1. Preheat the oven to 325°F. Thoroughly grease two 2-quart round ovenproof bowls.

2. Put the butter and sugar into a large bowl and beat with a handheld electric mixer until pale and creamy. Gradually beat in the eggs a little at a time. Sift together the flour and baking powder, then fold into the creamed mixture with the milk.

3. Divide the batter evenly between the prepared bowls, making a dip in the center with the back of a spoon (see step 3 photograph). Bake in the preheated oven for 50 minutes, then loosely cover each bowl with aluminum foil and bake for an additional 20–30 minutes, or until firm to the touch and a toothpick inserted into the center of the cakes comes out clean. Let cool in the bowls for 10 minutes, then turn out onto a wire rack to cool completely. Wrap the cold cakes in foil and chill in the refrigerator for 4–5 hours or overnight.

4. To assemble, cover a board with parchment paper. Level the top of each cake with a serrated knife. Scoop out the centers of the cakes, leaving a 1½-inch border (see step 4 photograph). Place one cake, cut side up, on the prepared board.

5. Spread some of the buttercream around the rim of the cake and pile the candies and half the colored sugar sprinkles into the center (see step 5 photograph). Invert the second cake on top to enclose the candies and make a globe-shape cake, pressing down gently to seal.

6. Using a spatula, spread a thin layer of buttercream all over the cake to secure any loose crumbs, then chill in the refrigerator for 1 hour. Spread the remaining frosting in a thick layer over the cake and decorate with the remaining sugar sprinkles.

3

4

5

Tip

For a more colorful frosting, beat in a little pink or yellow food coloring paste with the buttercream.

BIRTHDAY SURPRISE GIANT CUPCAKE

Celebrate a birthday in style with this supersized chocolate-flavor cupcake filled with a secret stash of candies.

 Serves 12 >> **Prep time:** 1 hr 10 mins, plus time to cool & chill >> **Cooking time:** 1 hr–1 hour 30 mins

⅓ cup unsweetened cocoa powder

⅓ cup boiling water

3 sticks butter, softened, plus extra for greasing

1½ cups firmly packed light brown sugar

6 extra-large eggs, beaten

2¾ cups all-purpose flour, plus extra for dusting

1½ teaspoons baking powder

To fill & decorate

1 quantity chocolate buttercream (see page 8)

confectioners' sugar, for dusting

1 pound blue ready-to-use fondant

1 pound mixed small candies, such as jelly beans and sugar-coated chocolate drops

You will also need

giant silicone cupcake mold

large pastry bag fitted with a medium star-shape tip

1. Preheat the oven to 325°F. Thoroughly grease the bottom and top of a giant silicone cupcake mold, then lightly dust with flour, tipping out any excess. Put both molds onto a baking sheet. Mix the cocoa powder and water together in a small bowl to make a smooth paste and set aside.

2. Put the butter and sugar into a bowl and beat together until pale and creamy. Gradually beat in the eggs, adding a spoonful of the flour if the mixture starts to curdle. Beat in the cocoa paste, then sift in the flour and baking powder and gently fold in, using a metal spoon. Divide the batter between the prepared molds, making a slight dip in the center of each.

3. Bake the top cake in the preheated oven for 1 hour–1 hour 15 minutes and bake the bottom cake for 1 hour 20 minutes– 1 hour 30 minutes, or until a toothpick inserted into the center of each cake comes out clean. Let cool in the molds for 10 minutes, then turn out onto a wire rack and let cool completely.

4. When the cakes are cold, wrap them in aluminum foil and place in the freezer for 30 minutes, or until firm.

5. Remove the cakes from the freezer and unwrap. Level the tops of each cake with a serrated knife. Carve out a large dip in the bottom cake, about 4 inches wide and 2½ inches deep (see step 5 photograph).

CONTINUED

5

6

8

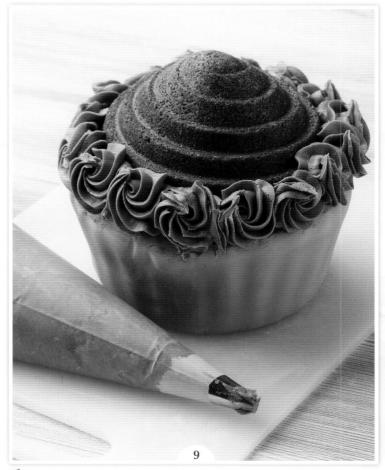

9

6. Place the bottom cake upside down on a board and spread a thin layer of the buttercream all over the cake. Lightly dust a surface with confectioners' sugar and roll out the fondant to an 11-inch circle. Drape the fondant over the bottom cake, smoothing it down firmly with your fingers (see step 6 photograph).

7. Carefully lift up the cake and place it upright on a board or flat plate. Trim off most of the excess fondant, leaving a ½-inch border. Fold in the border over the edge of the cake.

8. Fill the dip with the candies, reserving a few for decoration. Spread the edge of the bottom cake with a layer of buttercream (see step 8 photograph). Gently position the top cake on the bottom cake.

9. Spoon the remaining buttercream into a large pastry bag fitted with a medium star-shape tip. Pipe rosettes of buttercream all over the top of the cake to cover it completely (see step 9 photograph). Decorate with the remaining candies.

Tip

If your piping skills are not so good, simply swirl the chocolate buttercream over the top of the cupcake with a spatula and decorate with your choice of sugar sprinkles.

ICE CREAM CONE CUPCAKES

With a multicolor cake inside a crisp ice cream cone, these cheerful cupcakes are great for a sweet treat that won't melt too quickly on a hot sunny day.

Makes 12 >> **Prep time:** 25 mins, plus time to cool >> **Cooking time:** 20–25 mins

12 flat-bottom ice cream cones

1¼ sticks butter, softened

¾ cup granulated sugar

3 eggs, beaten

1¼ cups all-purpose flour

1¼ teaspoons baking powder

1 teaspoon vanilla extract

1 tablespoon milk

2 tablespoons sprinkles

To decorate
1 quantity buttercream
(see page 8)

12 mini chocolate bars (optional)

- - - - - - - - - - - - - - - - - - -

You will also need
12-section muffin pan

2 large pastry bags fitted with
a large star tip

1. Preheat the oven to 350°F. Stand the ice cream cones in a 12-section muffin pan (see step 1 photograph).

2. Put the butter and sugar into a bowl and beat together until pale and creamy. Gradually beat in the eggs, adding a spoonful of the flour if the mixture starts to curdle. Sift in the flour and baking powder and gently fold in, using a metal spoon. Fold in the vanilla extract and milk and nearly all the sprinkles (reserving 1–2 teaspoons for decoration).

3. Spoon the cake batter into a large disposable pastry bag and snip off the end. Pipe the batter into the ice cream cones, filling each one just over halfway full (see step 3 photograph).

4. Bake in the preheated oven for 20–25 minutes, or until risen, golden, and firm to the touch. Let cool in the pan for 10 minutes, then transfer to a wire rack and let cool completely.

5. To decorate, spoon the buttercream into a large pastry bag fitted with a large star tip. Pipe peaked swirls of buttercream on top of each cupcake (see step 5 photograph). Push a chocolate bar, if desired, into each swirl of buttercream and sprinkle with the reserved sprinkles.

Tip
Serve these cupcakes on the day of making because the ice cream cones will turn soft if they are kept for too long.

This edition published by Parragon Books Ltd in 2014 and distributed by

Parragon Inc.
440 Park Avenue South, 13th Floor
New York, NY 10016
www.parragon.com/lovefood

LOVE FOOD is an imprint of Parragon Books Ltd

ISBN 978-1-4723-5224-8

Printed in China

Project managed by Annabel King
Designed by Karli Skelton
Recipes and home economy by Angela Drake
Edited by Fiona Biggs
Photography by Clive Streeter

Notes for the Reader
This book uses standard kitchen measuring spoons and cups. All spoon and cup measurements are level
unless otherwise indicated. Unless otherwise stated, milk is assumed to be whole and eggs are large.

Garnishes, decorations, and serving suggestions are all optional and not necessarily included in the recipe
ingredients or method. The times given are only an approximate guide. Preparation times differ according
to the techniques used by different people and the cooking times may also vary from those given. Optional
ingredients, variations, or serving suggestions have not been included in the time calculations.

Picture acknowledgments:
Back cover image: Cake table © Tjitske van Leeuwen Photography/Getty Images